THE TURN FOR ITHACA

First published in 2026 by
The Dedalus Press
13 Moyclare Road
Baldoyle
Dublin D13 K1C2
Ireland

www.dedaluspress.com

ISBN 978-1-915629-50-0 (hardback)
ISBN 978-1-915629-51-7 (paperback)

Dedalus Press titles are available in Ireland
from Argosy Books (www.argosybooks.ie) and in the UK
from Inpress Books (www.inpressbooks.co.uk).

Cover image: 'A Friend for Fisher's Tree' (2012)
by Margaret Corcoran, watercolour and chalk
on paper, 31.5 x 37 cm, by kind permission.

Dedalus Press receives financial assistance from
The Arts Council / An Chomhairle Ealaíon.

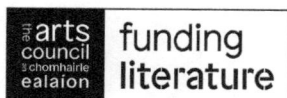

arts council / an chomhairle ealaíon — funding literature

THE TURN FOR ITHACA

GERARD SMYTH

DEDALUS PRESS

ACKNOWLEDGEMENTS

Many of these poems, or previous versions of them, were first published in the print and online publications: *Abridged, Agenda, Boyne Berries, Carnets du ShannOdet (Brittany), The Cormorant, Crannog, Cyphers, The High Window, The Irish Times, Kingdom Poets, New Humanist, The Manhattan Review, New Hibernia Review, Oxford Review, Poetry Ireland Review, Poetry People, Reading Ireland, Southword, Stony Thursday Book, The Stinging Fly, Studies, Temenos Academy Review, Waterford Healing Arts Poetry Postcards, Write Where We Are Now* (Poems written in lockdown, Manchester Metropolitan University 2020, ed. Carol Ann Duffy), *Where Love and Imagination Colour the Dark: Essays on Thomas Kinsella* (Wake Forest University Press, ed. Adrienne Leavy).

Also in the anthologies, *A Given Grace, an anthology of Christian poems* (Squircle Lines Press, Singapore); *Local Wonders: Poems of Our Immediate Surrounds* (Dedalus Press, ed. Pat Boran); *Romance Options: Love Poems for Today* (Dedalus Press, eds. Leanne Quinn and Joseph Woods); *Happy Birthday Mr Bob* (ed. Liamy Mac Nally); *Days of Clear Light, a Festschrift for Jessie Lendennie* (Salmon Poetry); *A Festschrift for Thomas McCarthy* (Southword) and *A Festschrift for Gerry Murphy* (Southword).

'In the Artist's Studio' was first published in the catalogue for Donald Teskey's exhibition, *Decade*, in the Royal Hibernian Academy Gallery in November 2022. 'An Irish Poet in Paris Yearns for Home' appeared in the limited edition *We Like It Here Beside the River* (Salvage Press); an early draft of 'The Book of Irish Wars' formed part of the sequence *After Easter* (Salvage Press limited edition, 2016). 'Isolation' was first published on the front page of *The Irish Times* and is included in the sequence *Plague Poems: A Leap Year* (Salvage Press, 2025). The Beechmount Ballroom was first published in *Navan: Its People and Its Past*. 'Ceol' was written for *Mícheál Ó Súilleabháin: A Life in Music* (Cork University Press). A number of these poems also appear in *The Haunted Radio* (Brighthorse Editions, St Paul, Minnesota, 2024).

Sincere thanks to Pat Boran and Raffaela Tranchino at Dedalus Press. Also to John F Deane, Thomas Dillon Redshaw, Aifric Mac Aodha, Annemarie Ní Churreáin, Dan Reardon, Grace Wilentz, James Harpur, Thomas McCarthy and Kerrie O'Brien for keeping the poetry conversation going.

Contents

⤳

Song of the Tortured Poet / 9

Building a City / 10

Dublin Ode / 12

An Irish Poet in Paris Yearns for Home / 14

Thomas Kinsella's Dublin / 15

Eavan Boland's Dublin / 16

Brendan Kennelly's Dublin / 18

Luke Kelly's Dublin / 19

City Prowler / 20

Brighton Square 1882 / 21

Fair City / 22

Broken Phone Box on Clanbrassil Street / 23

The Silent Era / 24

Reading Ilya Kaminsky / 25

The Next Country Will Be Closing Soon / 26

A Wrong Word / 27

My Back Pages / 28

The Man Who Talks to Cameras / 29

Closer Than We Imagined / 30

Isolation / 31

On the Fifteenth Sunday of a Plague Year / 32

Zoom / 33

The Haunted Radio / 34

First Funeral / 35

Under The Apple Tree / 36

Connolly Station / 37

Maggie's Grave / 38

Cloud-Watching In Roscommon / 39

Breakfast in Waterville / 40

Dinner with Ferlinghetti / 41

Dharma Bum / 42

Orpheus, Virgil and Dante / 43

In the Artist's Studio / 44

Lost Brother / 45

Hibbing / 46

Farmer's Daughter / 47

Ann Traynor's Field / 48

Ceol / 49

The Beechmount Ballroom / 51

Sergeant Pepper / 52

Beehive and Mascara / 52

When Bowie Died / 53

American Troubadour / 54

Growing a Beard to Look Like Che Guevara / 55

Catching the Ferry / 56

Waiting for St. Brigid's Day / 57

Many Mothers / 58

To a Son with Daughters / 59

Reading Pessoa on a Flight From Lisbon / 60

Listening to Ralph Fiennes Recite Eliot's Quartets / 61

Inhospitable Hostess / 62

The Republic of Duende / 63

The Good Reader / 65

My Father's House / 66

Like Byron's Daughter / 67

Astral Nights / 68

What The Young Saint Said / 69

Homage to Hartnett / 70

A Diptych of Days / 71

Blackboard, Chalk and Duster / 72

The Book of Irish Wars / 74

Tonight the Snowflakes, Tomorrow the Slush / 75

Minding the Shop / 76

Olympians / 77

Small Talk / 78

for Pauline

I have only what I remember
— W. S. Merwin

Song of the Tortured Poet

Has he squandered a life with the sullen art?
Let it become a habit,
were wasted words his treasury?
The morning verses, midnight nouns
and verbs crossed out, tossed away.
Was it all a cure for boredom –
a kind of servitude, a rapture
since poetry first appeared as a flutter in his ears?
Has he been unwise with the time he had,
writing stanzas that became a mask,
chasing ghost-sonnets, waiting on street corners
for an image to pass and stumble into his arms?
Sometimes there was barely a scribble
or nothing but a riddle on the page.
When others spent Sunday in the park
or hunted for the sound of the sea,
he stayed indoors and fine-tuned the melody,
listening for the reticent heartbeat
of an ode or elegy, wishing for one song
to add to a troubadour's repertoire.

Building a City

No city exists in the present tense, it is the only surviving mass-statement of our ancestors, and it changes inversely to its inhabitants. It is old when they are young, and when they grow old it has become amazingly and shiningly young again.
—James Stephens, Dublin novelist, poet and journalist

By stealth a city happens
on the maps and in the annals.
First settlers gather
where a town's born out of chance
and stays close to its river banks
until at last the traces of its genesis are gone –
clay and wattle are exchanged for wood,
wood replaced by stone: the building blocks
of castle tower, the chapel on ground
once dedicated to pagan gods.
Open spaces are colonised by those who build,
destroy and build again,
their settlements and sanctuaries
between the cess pits
and where the court of conscience sits.
Their gates and fences cannot repel
conqueror, neighbour, the carrier of plagues,
or the music that makes young girls
learn their first dance-steps.
There are laws and punishments,
all for the common good.
The cartographer comes and sketches
the many angles and the rough edges,
the graveyards and ghettoes
that are barely distinguishable.

He walks to the hillcrest to view the belfries
that one by one are heaven-sent.
On his map he draws the routes that wander
further from their source – the heartland
of the city where things get lost
for a thousand years: coins and combs,
the imprint of a house not found
until the city lights up its alphabet of neon.

Dublin Ode

There was the Liffy rolling downe the lea
—Edmund Spenser, 'Irish Rivers'

I always loved the city, its detours and divisions.
The lights when darkness falls on it.
The clocks, the bells, steeples, domes –
whatever makes us look to its horizons.

I always loved the city.
The summer rain on statues,
street-names that take the strain of history.
Rush hour and the hour
when the empty streets are cleaned.
The monuments weathered into myth.
Swans in the canal looking radiant.
The river knows its way from source to sea,
runs past the riverside church:
Eve and Adam among Franciscan saints.

I always loved the city. It began
with father's Sunday walk from bridge to bridge
and the one time that he crossed
to see the other side. The lights along the river
make the river look like it's playing with fire.
A Liffey-wind comes with the tide
to sharpen the aroma of brewing yeast.

I always loved the city, its lanes that lovers walk.
The lanes that were the short way home
for those old wives who lived so long they saw
Lord Nelson toppled from his pinnacle.

We like it here beside the river,
gulls like feathered Buddhas perch on walls of stone,
men digging for leaks discover
earth-smelling bones
buried since a battle or a famine or a plague.

An Irish Poet in Paris Yearns for Home

homage to Thomas MacGreevy

He was homesick for the white horse
on O'Connell Bridge,
the river flowing from hills of gorse,
the gulls that screeched high above the Post Office,
the statues that kept silent
but never could hide the hurt look
on each weather-beaten face.
He was homesick for *the midnight streets of Dublin
shiny in the rain*. Midnight rain
that hissed at the windows
of Law Library, Capuchin Friary,
the orphanage where crimes were hushed.
His city of claptrap and conspiracy,
of the unwritten sentence, the iambics of distress.
Crush of the crowds on Easter Sunday
watching the flag being raised, a wreath being laid,
fife and drum going down the street.
The city always waiting for great events –
city of disappointments,
nagging doubts, homespun sentiment.
A city he thinks he'll never see again
or smell its *stale voluptuousness*.

Thomas Kinsella's Dublin

in memory

We sat in the half-dark, never noticed dusk seeping in
from the Booterstown marsh.
We had a list of places to get through –
some of them gone from the map.
One of them, you said, was dust at your feet
when you returned with a friend but couldn't find
the beginning or end of Basin Lane
or the harbour where the barges once came with barley
to leave at the brew master's gate.
Further away, the old school was still there,
as solid as when you were learning to read
new words chalked on a blackboard.
So too was *The High Road* and *The Forty Steps*
where Cromwell's army slept
during a pause in the conquest.
In boyhood you found adventure ground:
a bridge, a river, brown water that *bubbled*
and poured at the end of Bow Lane.
Blood ran from the shambles, a pigyard
had troughs full of neighbourhood slops.
At the back of the shop where card players met,
an ancestor kept to her chamber –
(all this stayed in the memory and would not go away).
To get to city centre you had to walk the broad street
of history's defeats, past Emmet's *ghost scaffold.*
These were the places where first things happened.
Along the way you met the watchful and the watched,
and read the ground for 'local knowledge'.

Eavan Boland's Dublin

in memory

I was born in a place where rain is second nature
—Eavan Boland

It was a remembered city of wet umbrellas,
smoke from the chimneys, chimes from the steeples.
The last veterans were older by half a century
but as fervent as ever they were in the days of rebellion.
Fat pigeons perched on the statues of men
who stood on their plinths outside the halls
of rhetoric, close to Botany Bay.
It was a city of anomalies and contradictions,
enigmas and riddles. The street hawkers
set up their stalls next to the perfumed emporia.
The lights of Liberty Hall glimmered on Liffey water.
If you followed the bridges to the rivermouth,
the mailboat was waiting, ready to take the emigrant
out through the back door to London,
Manchester, Birmingham, Leeds.
On Grafton Street the era was changing,
the next generation making noises off-stage
in *The Bailey, O'Neills, Bewley's Café.*
It was before the renovation of Speranza's house.
Huguenot graves were hidden in a forgotten place.
In the remembered city of drizzle and downpour
secrets were safe, the ballads traditional
when sung in pub sessions on Saturday nights.
The buses were old, their numbers a code
to a clear destination out in the suburbs,
under the mountains, close to the sea
where the city was beginning to spawn new estates

and nobody heard of the patriots whose names
were given to the avenues, cul-de-sacs, smooth roads
where the stony roads had all disappeared.

Brendan Kennelly's Dublin

in memory

Those who wander are rarely lost:
good words planted on the T-shirt
worn by that girl stepping off the bus
into the flux of Nassau Street.
Light still fresh is creeping through the campus,
the college trees are coming into bloom,
cool greenness on their branches.
Sun breaking through to illuminate the gable end
of Finn's Hotel makes me pause to remember
this was where an epic began, a lustful romance.
Something's missing from the architecture.
Dawson Street looks bare.
There is a stranger at the poet's table –
the one who has vanished from the habitats
of Mangan, Clarke and Kavanagh,
disappeared from places where he liked to stroll
or stood transfixed in *the light on Portobello Bridge*.
He is gone to where he can *begin again*,
and taken with him his lilt and laugh
and words not written yet.

Luke Kelly's Dublin

for Des Geraghty, on his 80ᵗʰ birthday

Day after day the long boats came.
The boy with a biblical name
counted them in, counted them out.
He became a seeker of songs but never forgot
his holy ground where ship-light burned a hole in fog.
In barroom and porter house the week's wage
was lost, contraband sold and bought:
the bare knuckle fight, the midnight brawl
had a whiff of vinegar and salt.
Gone are the lanes that lovers walked,
the shortcut home, a way that zig-zagged after dark.
Gone too the men whose lungs were clogged,
whose hands were calloused.
They waited for the ships that carried songs.
Around their heads river-gulls cried out
a thanksgiving for what the river gave them
straight from its mouth. Down there
in the docklands it's the end of the road,
but the road is reborn as river water,
there's a bridge where the ferryman used to cross,
watched by the boy with a biblical name.

City Prowler

Fever-dazed he walks through a sleepwalker's oblivion
and through the alleys calling his *Dark Rosaleen.*

His hands stained with scrivener's ink,
his arms wearied by ledgers thick
with testaments kept on the highest shelf on York Street.

City prowler, he walks among the skinny dogs
of the dispossessed, passes a bleeding horse
on Camden Street, then a house of cholera
and a house ablaze with the light of many chandeliers.

His spirit *shipwrecked, befooled in love.....*
he dribbles the words of *The Nameless One.*
Behind him like a burning wheel the past is catching up.

City prowler, out looking for the tender care
of the opium nurse. Pity him, poor poet
with a head full of words that rhyme, who walks
through his lost worlds between Siberia and The Coombe.

Brighton Square 1882

A crooning father,
a mother who believed in miracles.
Between them in his cradle
a son already listening to the operatic arias
so often sung in Brighton Square.
He was the talk of the village,

of the tidy gardens, a child
born the second day of the second month,
No time was lost
taking him to the Christening font
where he saw his own reflection
and was spellbound by the image.

There was rejoicing in the square.
Neighbour watching neighbour
to see who would bring the first gift to his crib,
who would ask to hold him and whisper
in his ear *Out there you'll find your river,*
your city, the bedrock of your life.

Fair City

Where is Mecklenburgh Street
and Bella's pleasure house
that was there in the bygone?
The street was renamed. Bella moved on.
But when did this become a city like Gotham?
A city of vendettas, a combat zone
for public enemies. Each way we turn
there are posters of the missing.
The silver horse behind council flats
is a horse without grass ready to accept
the hand of kindness whenever it passes.
On a quiet street there's a chance
you'll be asked to hand over your money,
your phone, your watch, the ring
on your finger, wallet in your pocket.
Outside the General Post Office a tour guide
tells his flock to pause and see where the mob
put on a show, chanting the only chant they know,
rattling their slurs, spinning their lies
about the newcomers who think they're safe
when they arrive in Fair City.

Broken Phone Box on Clanbrassil Street

In the broken phone box on Clanbrassil Street
wires hang like dreadlocks from a Rastafarian's head.
This has been a vault of silence since the wires were cut,
all the old conversations under the dust.
A voice here could harmonise with a voice from far away.
Calls were made to save a life, seek forgiveness,
confess to shame or sometimes send a tear-stained cry
for help that never came. The book of numbers
has been torn to bits, pages blow into the street.
The stuttering tongue said *Please come home.*
The voice in a rage shouted *Never return.*
Once in a while it rang and somebody passing by
stepped inside to ask: *Who is this, where are you calling from?*

The Silent Era

Now we have the witness statements,
have found the hidden graves in lonely places.
Now the orphans are not afraid to speak,
the stolen child has come back to trace her roots.
We no longer live in the silent era
and know who to blame and who should feel shame
in the old school, under the convent bell,
in the icy asylum for daughters in distress,
its brick and stone saturated with their sweat.
Kept out of sight scrubbing the sheets,
they missed the time of their lives, the nostalgia years.
O Magdalene your name sounds feather-light
but it bears the weight of crimes
far heavier than Judas's betrayal of Christ.

Reading Ilya Kaminsky

Between Akhmatova and Mandelstam
there is bookspace on the shelf for the poet from Odesa.
I must follow his verses back to where they sprang from
like the first green shoots that rise out of the snow.
I must follow him back to his city of ancestors
where his bloodline ran
and all the old buildings were bleached in the sun.
These poems of his look me in the eye,
they are like a stiff breeze from the Black Sea.
I hold them to my ear and hear a polka.
It is music no bombardment can silence or kill,
no persecution can suppress with weaponry.
Just as in the days of early autumn
when it is time to rake the leaves, it's time again
to read the poet from Odesa, turn his pages
and hope to find a poem with a happy ending
in which I hear a beckoning shout from *Pushkin Street*.
Or one with wheat fields and a sunflower farm,
a grandmother making jam
with plums stolen from the highest branches.

The Next Country Will Be Closing Soon

Those who leave in a hurry leave behind
things forgotten in the rush,
the embroidered scarf,
the bible belonging to a grandmother
who never got further than Genesis.
Those who leave in a midnight dash
should prepare to swim,
don't know where they're heading
and don't care so long as the road ahead
takes them somewhere else,
preferably daylight in the west.
Those who leave must say *Goodbye*
to the loyal dog, the canary,
the cat with six lives gone.
They cannot carry everything,
must choose between a family heirloom
and the new violin
a precocious child has been learning to play.
They will fall many times,
have sleepless nights,
receive a slap in the face to keep them awake.
Those who can't run never catch up
with the quick and the swift who have no time to rest
because it is said
the next country will be closing soon.

A Wrong Word

or irony misunderstood,
a wayward thought, a question
whispered in a low voice.

That's all it takes to offend the ministry,
for the jailer to shackle the hand that writes,
smash to splinters a poet's limbs,
make him dig the pit into which he disappears,
stripped of everything except his conscience.

A wrong word, a joke, a parable,
a poem that's allegorical.

That's all it takes for banishment,
to be marched through blizzard, snow drift,
under a blistering sky, sent next to nowhere
by the killers of language,
those who decide who's next to vanish

for *one mistake, a slip of the tongue,*
the unintended adjective.

My Back Pages

for Gerry Murphy

Looking through old news I skip the years
of Ayatollahs and moving statues,
of changes in the ozone, ghost factories,
an unmanned voyage to the galaxies.
I avoid the long reports of a propaganda speech,
the years when headlines cried for peace
or declared a rise in civil disobedience,
that summer rain had spoiled the crops.
Asylum-seekers on the beaches of Europa
look like extras on the set of *Exodus*.
Fact and falsehood are close to one another.
New contagions discovered in places
with tongue-twisting names.
Day after day more of the same:
Mrs T closing the pits of Yorkshire and Wales.
The summer of black armbands
and black flags hanging over towns and farms.
Then the news from Tiananmen Square
when Tiananmen Square was the address
for the revolution quenched like a flame:
that image of David and Goliath
will haunt me forever. A war photographer's
camera is never empty – always one more
bombed-out hospital, a school in rubble,
zealots with their faces covered.
How thin they look, the fashion models,
the bashful princess with nowhere to hide.
But the poet smiles –
he has just come home with his Nobel Prize.

The Man Who Talks to Cameras

He is always there, the man who talks to cameras,
always first to land where something bad happens –
war, disaster, *coup d'état,*
the results of tragic circumstance.

He stands in rubble, in the ashes, in the flood.
a serious look on his face,
announcing to the world that the world's gone mad.

He lives a life of *déjà-vu,* chancing his luck
in the danger zone, in the noise of conflict,
the city under attack and burning like Carthage.

He is there for deadlock, breakthrough, crisis at noon.
Always around when the digging is done
and the missing are found
or the long siege ends and the dead are counted.

Sometimes he begins with a quote from Gandhi.
The last time he was seen
he was standing with his back to Sniper Alley.

Closer Than We Imagined

The summer was covered in Chernobyl dust.
We worried that the September berries might poison us,
that the newborn would have no tears to cry.

We waited for news from the danger zones,
paid better attention to which way the wind was blowing.
The shock of what happened got into our dreams.

We watched for sickness, some new disease
and watched each other for signs;
irregular heartbeat, burning cheeks.

No one would taste the honey or pull up the weeds.
The chimney sweep refused to clean the chimney.
We were amazed when mountain sheep were still alive

after weeks of eating grass laced with rain
from thick black clouds that came
from a country that was closer than we imagined.

Isolation

Bunched together like a gathering tribe,
the daffodils rise again and there are signs
of sun behind the clouds.
We still have bread and books
and songs to keep the radio alive.
A note through the door is a kind surprise
and birds on the branches
of the trees outside stay up late.
The mornings are not so dark,
the internet takes us to the works of art,
tunes us in to Debussy or Paul Simon,
brings us close to the faraway country
where loved ones are.
A kite above someone's back garden
rises and dips and gives a moment of joy
to a face in the window of isolation.

March 17ᵗʰ–19ᵗʰ, 2020

On the Fifteenth Sunday of a Plague Year

On the fifteenth Sunday of a plague year
we count the sparrows one by one as they appear.
The garden's a jukebox of songbirds and songs.
They have returned to treetop, clothesline,
the bush of thorns. Unseen but not unheard
the blackbird stays well hidden in the ivy on the wall,
but the magpie on the roof of the shed
is bully and thief and neighbour from hell.
Like childhood hurts the short days are behind us.
First light at sunrise is the last trick of the night.
It is too much to say that even in bad times
we have heavenly days, an excess of peace?
The marching band cancelled, no parade,
no flag-waving, no oration or orator waiting for applause.
The fifteenth Sunday of the year is spent with swans
on the shaded banks of the canal
where a stranger packed his tent and moved on.
No one saw him rise and go, hopefully to where
there is goodwill and not where harm is done.

Zoom

The greatest poverty is not to live in a physical world
—Wallace Stevens

We criss-cross in the virtual world.
You from the west, I from the east,
all of the others have disappeared.
No handshakes or kiss on the cheeks
but we wave like the actor in a walk-on part.

You have the sunsets but I see the dawn
while you're still in the dark.
Behind my back an arrangement of books
including some I borrowed but never returned,
some I open when I am lost for words.

In the virtual world the walls are thin,
the look on our faces is *bear it and grin*.
Without leaving home we become nomadic
and drop into view in a faraway kitchen
where we listen more than we speak.

for Mary O'Malley

The Haunted Radio

So many friends have gone to dwell in the haunted radio.
Some had no time for a last farewell,
some left in the dark thinking they'd be back.

One still had the smell of sweetened coffee on her breath,
a story half-read fell from her lap.
They have gone with their heartaches and worst mistakes,

but also every gladness that they had.
Some with their love of Chopin and Bach,
the metaphors in Shakespeare's sonnets, Eliot's *Waste Land*.

Some left us when the fields were sinking deeper
into August grass, when a song we heard all summer
was dropping down the charts.

And then those others who blackened our festival of mirth,
who were lost to us in the chill
of the twelfth month, as if they discovered a vanishing trick.

First Funeral

Doors were closed with a gentle pull,
the grown-ups whispered or were struck dumb.
It was a day he didn't go to school, day of his first funeral.

That night he dreamed he was with the dead
whose wounds and scars had disappeared,
whose broken hearts were healed.

One came and put her arms around him, called him Son.
But then another pointed back
to where he came from, the door he'd entered.

Under The Apple Tree

At three o'clock in the school yard
she saw her first eclipse of the sun.
At six o'clock when the news came on
she heard there could be a war,
that both sides had the nuclear bomb.
At a dance in the local hall
the moral guardians kept watch
for one wrong step, the length of a dress,
the colour of lipstick or a tightening hold
unacceptable to them.
All her anniversaries came and went.
Then one year on the date of her birth
she noticed she was wearing her father's frown,
her mother's wearied countenance.
Now her life is under the apple tree
where someone has heaped her worn-out shoes,
her keepsakes and souvenirs,
postcards showing the Cliffs of Moher,
candles of Fatima,
flamenco dancers in a Spanish taverna.
In her heyday she was always first to sing
in any gathering of those she loved
or among mourners
when the maudlin talk broke in.
She was one of the few
who could sing an aria and make it spin
upwards to the higher altitudes.

Connolly Station

On the escalator in Connolly Station
a tap on the shoulder made me turn to face him
and shake his hand – a friend
I hadn't seen for years
not since he and I wore skinny jeans.
Tears in his eyes, tears on his sleeve –
he said he had been reading *The History of Grief.*
Blinded by the sun of a distant summer
he and I lost each other in the great escape
when school days finished.
How old he looked, even older than his mother
who was still alive and stood beside him
flicking a silver hair from his coat.
Once he had great expectations
of finding Utopia at the end of the street.
It wasn't there, only a world colder and emptier
than the roads on Christmas morning.
That evening in May on the Connolly escalator
we counted the years we let slide,
made a promise to keep in touch,
knowing we wouldn't, that this was just random
chance, finding each other again.

Maggie's Grave

On a day when the coast of Skerries looks like heaven
and those mountains that *sweep down to the sea* stand unclouded
I go looking for your name and find it on a hilltop
where the flowers are blown away
from the graves of village entertainers, widows of drowned sailors,
the fishermen who used to come back in the evening
with the silver of their catch.
Their days were all the same, a kind of misty rain
through which they saw the still world of a distant peninsula.
Their week was spent attentive to the sea
but anticipating Sunday on *terra firma*.
On a day when every shade of green looks greener,
when sea and headland appear God-given
I go looking for your name, climbing to a place
where those the healer could not save
lie safe from the storms above them.

Cloud-Watching In Roscommon

for Al and Mary Cunningham

There is a landscape that might hold clues
to the beginning of time.
Its archaeology outwits the archaeologist
who pokes around in the rain-soaked sunshine.
When a day breaks with no shadow on the lakes
and the sky seems affable
we decide on a walk, but before stepping out
clouds gather, the morning turns dark,
the wet hills become a vista half-vanished.
Up where the mines are closed, a gale rises
like fits of laughter, the scenic routes are misty,
the pass impassable
and the ruins of antiquity are rattling.
The rain never stops. It takes us into a trance
repeating those rhythms it makes on stone walls,
the roadside shrines and Celtic cross.
We cloud-watch and wait for the drops to fall,
first a few, then the deluge that is unstoppable.

Breakfast in Waterville

for Paddy and Fíona

In a breakfast room on the edge of Europa
the early riser eats alone,
a guest who sits with his back to the view –
a postcard scene when the sky is clear.

The morning light regains its ground.
A hazy sun builds the day out of nothing.
Mountains take shape, roads appear,
landmarks grow into clear definition.

The songs that were sung last night
and the tunes of the accordion player
were sung and played as if gods were listening
and angels too, ready to dance on the head of a pin.

It is daybreak in Waterville, everything calm
until another Atlantic storm blows in,
pounding the Prince of Clowns who stands
as we remember him on the silent screen.

A man who should have stayed home
is walking the beach with his dog.
The two of them could rise and blow far away,
if not as far as Finisterre, at least to Derrynane.

The clouds move faster, waves kick harder
on the shore where the mariner-poet
knocked on the imaginary door
and let out his Milesian roar of ecstatic poetry.

Dinner with Ferlinghetti

for Pat Boran

It was one of those evenings bright as day.
Beer in our glasses, bones on our plates
and in my jacket pocket Ferlinghetti's
Coney Island of the Mind.

The poet himself sitting on the opposite
side of the table looked like an avatar
or sultan of jazz, the elder among us
he was mostly listening to the chitchat and gossip,
but in his silence might have been thinking
of Ginsberg and Corso, their heyday gone
with the golden age of hipster and flower child.

But that night we dined we spoke about
Dedalus the father and Dedalus the son
and where in the city he could find their ghosts.
We could hear a river and saw through a window
a fox cub running into the foliage.
It slipped my mind to ask about Coney Island –
the high excitement of riding the Wonder Wheel.

Dharma Bum

Kerouac said he saw his visions in newsreel grey:
his scenes from boyhood, a lost brother
who stayed in his dreams,
his own shadow running at speed on a football field
where he became a hero in the league.
Nothing could stop his dance
to the rhythms, the beats of typewriter jazz.
Kerouac said that leaving a childhood house
was *a catastrophe of the heart* ...
And he knew about that, so many impermanent
addresses between Moody Street and Ozone Park.
He worshipped Thomas Wolfe and Lester Young,
the bebop he heard in Harlem clubs.
A long drive took him to a heaven of the mind:
the earthly delights of Panama Street,
Mexican sunlight, a bottle of Skid Row wine.

Orpheus, Virgil and Dante

Bereft of its great poets
our old world's in darkness.
—Michael Hartnett, after the Irish of Ó Bruadair

Poets are dying
leaving other poets to mourn and compose
the requiem, eulogy, elegy
and the mean words of jealousy
in a posthumous review.
Poets are dying, leaving verses unfinished,
rough drafts that are puzzles
and some poems of their youth still unexplained.
Poets are dying,
their last scribbles will remain in the pockets
of coats for resale in the charity shops.
Poets are dying, their names will be lost
in second-hand anthologies, books with a theme
that belongs to the past.
Poets are dying, the maker of strict rhymes
who for ten years brooded on six lines.
Another was versatile with the sonnet,
won the prizes, ignored the mockers.
The underworld is filling up and Orpheus
grows impatient at the number of times
he must open the gates
and check the names with Virgil and Dante.

In the Artist's Studio

for Donald Teskey

This is where the kingfisher hides.
Trees stand like children petrified with fright.
The sparrow hawk is always to blame
and here on this riverbank
it's as if someone came and turned bread into stone.

Two rivers, one running low, neither can sleep
until they reach the seabed and then they might dream
of Beaver Row and Crum Creek.
The buddleia in bloom grows lush as Arcadia.
By the repetitious weir listen, you'll hear
the slick gush of water that comes from Kippure.

As Charles Wright says in his May Journal
Notes from the provinces always start with the weather.
So too the sketch of an island in the west,
its ridgeline rising from Blacksod Bay
where land and tide are like sister and brother,
side by side haunting each other.

When you can't find the right word a colour will do
to describe the places that flourish and wither,
the come-and-go of footprints in snow, the backstreets
of Paris or Gougane Barra where, it is said, Saint Finbarr
heard the song of the wren in the valley.

Lost Brother

in memory of Eugene Smyth, July–August 1950

I found you at last, lost brother,
in among the many whose silence
is the same in every language.
It was as if we stumbled into one another
when I checked for your name in the cemetery ledger.
For years your absence has been stalking me.
Because you died in infancy
you could not be recorded in scrapbook or album.
You were a passerby who left shadows
with nobody in them,
who never heard the bells of Sunday morning
when the half-dead rise again.
You never joined hands with another or waywardly danced,
never feared drowning while learning to swim,
felt the gash made by thorns, sting of a wasp,
or went down to the harbour at evening
to watch the outgoing tide –
its vanishing trick that leaves a dark stain, opens a void.

Hibbing

in memory of Gerry Dawe

I see you, a kid in Belfast, listening to Luxembourg,
reading James Baldwin and Carson McCullers.

I see you wearing your Ban-the-Bomb badge
on a Saturday march down Royal Avenue,

a black armband worn in homage
when Otis Redding died in a crash.

I see you on Nun's Island, at Moon's Corner –
the Sixties are over, there's blood on the tracks.

You told us things were not good in your mother city,
that somebody there turned out the lights.

I see you walking the promenade of Asylum Harbour,
the pier where you took in sea air in blustery weather

or stood to catch a glimpse of the slow-moving ferry.
I hear you telling me you're heading to the prairie

and its wide open sky, that Hibbing's on your list
of places to visit when you arrive.

Maybe take a *Greyhound*, you said,
if one was going that way from St Paul.

Because Hibbing was where another North Country Boy
heard the first chords of his continuous song.

Farmer's Daughter

All day she preferred to be on open ground,
not looking for dust in corners of the house,
but out calling the hens or cutting the nettles.

First thing in the morning she walked the fields
to see the fresh dew, the flourishing grass.
All day she knew she must give the poor beast

its last meal before the pig killer came,
to make his deal, seal it with a spit;
the money in his pocket had pig's blood on it.

She had bad dreams of hay rotting in meadows,
an animal sick, one of the heifers
or the cow that always gave plenty of milk.

She felt she was rich because she had
all that mattered – a few small fields of the parish,
a roof, her ramshackle yard.

Now and then she brought flowers from the bog.
And for Sunday night she had dancing shoes
to make her feel transformed.

Ann Traynor's Field

I found the poems in the field, and only wrote them down
—John Clare

It was a field bearing the name of a woman
as many do when they are in a woman's keeping.
But Ann Traynor's field is nowhere now
except written down in folklore.
It has been nibbled away but once it was there,
like a theatre where the shadows of evening used to play.
Sometimes it was the earth beneath the feet
of sower and reaper, its rebirth certain
between April and May.
A place where the crows would gather
to pester a grazing herd.
March hares ran through it in wild commotion.
It was unremarkable, a grassy patch,
though that was before the thistles took over
after the battle between thistle and clover.
It was once divided but reunited by legal argument,
the law of possession.
A gap in the hedge was entry and exit.
The gate that sagged was many times mended
before it vanished.

for Belinda Quirke

Ceol

1. THE HOUSE ON THE COOMBE

Passing that house we wanted to dance.
Music came out of the walls at night –
tunes that were buried and dug up again.
A lullaby for the newborn, dozing and swaddled
in the lying-in hospital a few doors away.

The first notes were barely audible,
reticent as morning sun behind morning cloud.
Then the sound of a crowded house,
the clear run of a long finish that kept circling
and circling but never settling on ground.

There was story-telling when the music stopped
for a sip, a swig, a cigarette under the moon.
One sad neighbour always dropped in
when she heard the tin whistle beginning its dirge.

The last fling went on and on
until the morning chill when the milkman came
with his bottles of milk, and stars were gone
from the sky above St Catherine's Clock.

2. THE ROAD FROM NOBBER

The first rhythms he heard rang clear in his father's forge:
hammer on anvil, stress of the chisel, clatter of tongs.

He knew only by touch what others could see:
his smallpox scars, the dripping rain,
sun glinting on glass, frost in the air
on the first cold morning
when the strings of his harp became bad-tempered.

When he started his travels, his walking stick was cut
from a tree that grew between salt sea air and mountain drizzle.
Some women were trouble –
Fanny Power and *Eleanor Plunkett.*

And when he grew tired of hearing them say *Play us that tune,*
he took up his instrument and moved on
to wherever a lord of the manor might pay for a planxty
to rouse his guests, make them drum the bare boards
with their quicksteps, warm the cold air of his house.

The Beechmount Ballroom

Dance first, think later
—Samuel Beckett

One snatch of song is all it takes
and she is back in *The Beechmount Ballroom*,
back in the throng, feeling the quick vibrations

or hearing the melodies that were more serene –
the clarinet solo, the singer with the sheen
of sweat pouring down his cheeks.

The lights were like lights in harbour fog
and when the musicians rolled up their sleeves
to play a faster song, some girl always fainted.

The shy ones huddled against the wall,
or in a corner shuffling their feet until the last dance,
(a late request to slow the tempo).

That was the moment to lean a little closer
to whoever was close, before the evening
became a myth, the doorman let the cold air in.

Sergeant Pepper

Mindblowing was the word we heard
when the disc stopped spinning, lost its voice.
Slipped from its sleeve, it became a wonder in our hands –
the unimagined *Lonely Hearts Club Band.*

Bought with shillings saved through weeks of thrift
it is now the souvenir of our days of looking into mirrors,
of another bygone *Annus Mirabilis*
but not the one Larkin named, his warm-up year
of '63 when the action started,
the years ahead like strawberry fields to be harvested.

Beehive and Mascara

It's not the songs she sang,
not even *Son of a Preacher Man,*
that we remember most,
but how she looked:
her beehive and mascara,
the blush we couldn't see
on the black-and-white TV screen.

When Bowie Died

When Bowie died the *News at Ten*
showed a line of tear-stained Bowie fans,
comrades-in-arms singing the verses
of *Ashes to Ashes, Life on Mars.*
They were building a shrine to Ziggy Stardust,
unfurling a flag with his portrait from the golden years.
That night the war on terror was low on the list.
The fall of statesmen hardly mattered.
It seemed as if the moon gave extra moonlight
for his long haul to whatever planet a Starman travels to
passing through Potsdammer Platz,
through the flash of paparazzi cameras.
It was dead of winter in Manhattan,
snow on the autobahn when Bowie died
leaving us with his requiem for Lazarus.

American Troubadour

for Jessie Lendennie

When the show was over, the man who shouted *Judas*
disappeared, but what he said was written
into the annals. The troubadour went on,
covering his tracks so that no one could catch him
by collar or cuff. No pause for rest,
harmonica hanging from his neck.
One hand on the bible, the other deciding
between Shakespeare, Homer, *Leaves of Grass*.
Southbound. Northbound. Bound to his purpose:
the climb to Parnassus,
harder to reach than Louisiana, Tulsa, Kansas.
Sometimes he calls himself Jack Frost,
gets caught in the weave of words from his loom,
saying under his breath *Never could drink that blood
and call it wine.*
Close up the half-smile shows its cracks.
On stage it sometimes falls from his mask.

Growing a Beard to Look Like Che Guevara

riff on a line by Deryn Rees-Jones

To be twenty and begin again!
Listening to Ray Davies on a sunny afternoon.
Walking home in the hush of a Sunday morning,
too early for the Sunday bells
that always seem to know just when
to begin their arias. *To be twenty and begin again!*
Dusting off the ashes of a first romance
but happy to watch the sunrise
with that girl who is reading Jean-Paul Sartre.

To be twenty and begin again! A day tripper
on the magic bus, writing love poems
with only a hint of who the beloved is.
Hot-blooded like a son of Zeus,
strolling the boulevard from Nassau Street
to the gates of the park where the city's young
have their dominion on the urban grass.

To be twenty and begin again! A daytime sleeper.
Night sailor on the ship of news.
Never a day without music, the needle in the grooves.
To be twenty and begin again! Growing
a beard to look like Che Guevera.
Ban the bomb our marching song, our mantra.

Catching the Ferry

for Simon

The night before we sailed,
we stopped in Wales
in a guesthouse good enough
for one night only.
The room was out-of-date.
The furniture and furnishings
were vintage 1910.
The nylon sheets crackled
when we lay down on them.
It was hard to breathe
in the dusty evening heat
trapped between the four walls
and the ceiling.
The all-night coming and going
and pushing at the door
was as sinister as that movie
made by Hitchcock in his heyday.
The sound of the dumb waiter
started early in the morning.
The breakfast plates held breakfasts
cooked the day before.
Our waitress had the shakes,
dropped cigarette ash onto the table
and told us it was raining,
that it always rained in Wales,
in the valleys, on the peaks.
We quickly took the wet roads out
to where the Irish Sea was waiting.

Waiting for St. Brigid's Day

On a day like this, frost on the ground,
a cold fog wrapped around the house
I look for an image to unfreeze the spirit:
Montale's sunflower, Kavanagh's bluebells
found when he stopped on his way through Meath.
In the recovery room wounds are deep
and counted by the dozen. On a day like this
a white sun disappears soon after it has risen.
And even though it's still the darkest month,
ice on the roads, a snow crown topping that hill
we call mountain, I think of our February harbinger
of fine spring days whose name the holy
wells were given
and will keep until their last trickle.
She could save a house from burning,
a boat from sinking,
tell the difference between magic and miracle.

Many Mothers

I had many mothers, all of them schooled me
in far more than the rudimentary.
One made me a reader of books,
fitted my feet into new shoes.
Every Saturday one took me to Woolworths
to pick and choose from the counter of sweets.
Another washed my clothes every Monday
and hung them to dry,
billowing together because the morning was gusty.
I don't remember, can only guess,
but I think my first mother once nursed me
from sickness to health, and walked me to school
before I could go there on my own.
One combed my hair and gave it a side-split
that never again was as straight as when she created it.
One showed me the way to hold a pen,
steadied my hand as it ran through the alphabet.
She was under the spell of her spool of thread
when mending the trousers I tore on the fence.
One bought me playthings and puzzles,
a spinning top that never stopped spinning.
The one with a godmother's smile
took me to her favourite shrines –
Our Lady of Dublin, St Valentine.
Her murmurings made a sound
like fingertips on musical strings.
I had many mothers but one by one pushed them away.

To a Son with Daughters

for Karl

I watch you now in your fatherhood
and not as the son I had, asleep in your safe
harbour, dressed in your night-armour.
I watch you now in your fatherhood,
a daughter on your shoulders,
a daughter in your arms.
I see you joining the dots, solving the puzzles.
Some day the magic kingdom
will have no magic left.
But it's too soon yet to put that weight
on their shoulders while they're still amazed
by magic tricks, still playing with sand
on sandy beaches, asking for stories
that are far-fetched. So for now at least,
Lady Macbeth can wait in the wings,
Antigone stay home with the Greeks.
Two sisters playing you like an instrument.
Soon they'll discover that beneath the waves
there's a Lost Atlantis, there'll be questions
needing honest answers ....

Reading Pessoa on a Flight From Lisbon

Between Finisterre and the Bay of Biscay
the stillness of flight is a mystery.
I'm reading Pessoa, the page open
on *Solemn Over Fertile Country* –
but that's Ricardo Reis, another prince of sadness
and *saudade*, from the land of old cathedrals.

I turn to the metres of *The Keeper of Sheep*,
then a poem in which the King of Portugal appears.
This poet has *more souls than one*,
souls washed in the rain of Lisbon.
I close a page, open another:
Pessoa the mystic is waiting there, so he and I

travel on, trusting our guides,
mechanical power and gravity's pull –
and just as the engine's voice goes deep,
roars out a hymn to *the sorrowful universe*,
we are told to prepare for the long descent;
the balancing act, the illusion of stealth.

Listening to Ralph Fiennes Recite Eliot's *Quartets*

for Christine Monk

Actor, script, two empty chairs,
light filling the space between them.
The stage could be a country no one visits.
Not only with his voice
but with his hands making signs,
he reveals to us the verses of a tragic mind
brooding on the enigma of time,
past, present and eternal.
Sometimes he must say the same thing twice,
let his tongue play with a poet's philosophies.
No one comes to wipe his brow
or say *Stop now*, so he goes on,
never giving up or giving in.
We are on the way to Little Gidding.
In order to arrive, we make digressions,
crossing gloomy hills,
a river he believes is a strong brown god.
Who among us would dare to stand and shout,
crying out *No it's not* or contradict any thought
the Muses brought to Eliot's table.

Inhospitable Hostess

In Moscow once, in the month of summer snow,
five of us entered the house of Marina Tsvetayeva,
but first we stood outside repeating her name
to get it right, speak it like a Muscovite.
And then our host allowed us in, led us from room
to room, pausing at a door or on a stair
to talk about the intimations of her presence,
tell us where her souvenirs came from:
Paris, Berlin, Prague…
It was a house she once shared with the *Muse of Lament*.
The furniture showed its age and in every photograph
a knowing look on Marina's face.
One among us noticed that all her books
were still in place, some musky from the years,
some that seemed so fresh
we could have been in the forest with the trees.
Her hour of need took years on the Russian clock.
Each time we got new information
the five of us would nod
and think of her, Marina Tsvetayeva,
young woman in an old dress, inhospitable hostess…

The Republic of *Duende*

for Thomas McCarthy

1. A PHOTOGRAPH OF ANTONIO MACHADO

The Republic is dying, or already dead,
the spirit of Guernica under rubble and blood
but even in war, on the eve of exile,
Machado is a poet of style, looking his best,
a homburg crowning his head, *grand senor*
of *Duende* leaning on his walking stick.
The look on his face is the look of a man
who has witnessed things falling apart
as he walked through Madrid, Seville, Barcelona.
He is seated serenely, *the scent of absence*
around him. Over his shoulder, out of focus,
a snapshot of the poet who would never look old:
Lorca by then a ghost in Granada,
a ghost on the road nobody knows.

2. LORCA'S BONES

There is no guided tour to Lorca's grave.
Because there's no body, no bones, no trace
of the poet's broken remains.
Wherever they are they need to be raised
from the dust and reburied with an epitaph
to explain why it took so long.
The bullfighters of Cordoba might come
to pay homage, light candles, spread a blanket
of the flowers he loved
There could be drumbeats, flamenco, even a tango,

silent prayers, a cry of distress.
The gypsy music of Andalusia is the only imperative.
A guest from Havana and the Mayor of New York
could sit side by side and discuss
the meaning of *Yerma*.
The first to remember will stand up and speak
words chosen from Machado's lament
for the poet last seen *flirting with death*.

The Good Reader

in memory of Eileen Battersby

When I asked where she came from,
I heard her say *California*
as if that place close to the sun
was a storyteller's fiction.
Late for everything but always forgiven,
she could read a long Russian
novel between dusk and dawn,
then read it again and finish by noon.
Fictions, fables, tales out of school
burnished by a biographer's pen.
She lived in the mind of Thomas Mann,
Kafka, Steinbeck, John McGahern.
A book bag of stories swaddled in her arms –
Southern Gothic or set in the Jazz Age
of misfits, hedonists, all chasing paradise.
Dog rescuer too and friend of the stray,
she could name the antiquities of the Boyne,
the horses that died and the ones
that survived the Great War.
Black Beauty taught her
Man is the source of all grief.
On December twenty-first,
chill of the solstice across the plains of Meath,
she waited for sunrise, its buttery light
like fresh paint on the walls of Newgrange.

My Father's House

.....*Let me try to recall*
What building stood here. Was there a building at all?
—James Merrill

For years I watched its decline and fall.
First there was a crack in the wall, then a hole in the roof.
The crack moved from room to room,
the hole grew and gave a better view
of the dark clouds and touch of blue.

One day I turned to look and it was gone.
I felt a sudden nostalgia for the floors of cold linoleum,
the tell-tale step that creaked in the hall,
the shuddering pipes, the window where my father sat
reading the crimes of Agatha Christie.

In winter he watched the way the wintry sun
came in to light the dusty surfaces,
illuminate the bones of his late-night feast,
the stack of newspapers at his feet,
one for each day of the week, one for every catastrophe.

But the time came when nobody was home,
the stove unlit, the chimney cold.
One day the house was gone
but left a scar on that corner of the old town,
a meagre space when you look at it now.

for my sister Anne

Like Byron's Daughter

On the night of the eclipse she lured him
with her astronomer's knowledge
of Venus and the planets.
She took him to the observatory,
told him she could magnify the stars.

Their arrangement was to meet when the sun
went down, out Finglas way.
But the sky was charcoal with clouds of rain
and the promise she made
was impossible to keep.

Like Byron's daughter, it was her belief
that science was making the old beliefs
obsolete, or so she said
that night they searched the Milky Way
but couldn't find her starry crown,

no primal flash among the galaxies
or signs to tell of the yet-to-be,
what they might become.
That night the sky was Dead End Street.
He wished her happiness and luck.

Astral Nights

for Joe Smith

Once, out in a country field at night,
I saw stars in numbers I could not count,
constellations held in balance:
some only birthing, some close to extinction.
There was moonshine on the billowing grass
and on stubble that remained after the harvest.
Was it all by chance, a cosmic accident?
That summer night I was too young to ask
a question so profound,
but looking at the firmament, standing in clover,
I sensed that it was still the sixth day of creation,
the gardener still cultivating
root and branch of the Tree of Knowledge;
his fingerprints on every fossil,
his radiance renewing itself with every supernova.

What The Young Saint Said

for John F Deane

Let God be God, the young saint said,
not Roman, not Greek,
or belonging only to pilgrim and conqueror
but the God of all things: the Judas Tree
and hornet's nest, songthrush and garden slug.

Let God be God, not the bearer of so many names
or the judge who sits in the court of angels.
Let him not be the gatekeeper at the Gates of Wrath,
the tormenter of an innocent conscience.

Let God be God, the young saint said,
not the cause of holy wars
or one who sends his proxies to rob our mirth
but a God unbothered by heresies of dogma,
His presence heard in the singer's voice,
sound of the orchestra, the iron gate
when it creaks, the bells on Paternoster Street.

Homage to Hartnett

for Aifric Mac Aodha

He was the Captain of Joyce's Tower
but decided enough was enough
of the Anglo-Saxon curse,
knocked back what was left in his glass,
walked out with a wave of farewell
and a master plan to bring fire to the ashes
of a seldom-spoken language.

From Granada he brought back
Lorca's gypsy ballads.
When the blackbird whistled
in Croom and Camas he was there to listen,
a naturalist, a new and living Ó Rathaille.

In Kensington, on the underground
where nobody looks at anyone else
he looked ascetic. And on Leeson Street,
in the Saturday crowd he was there again,
striking a match: the haiku-master
of Emmet Road wedged between *Sweet
Afton* and *Woodbine* smoke.

A Diptych of Days

1

We called it the day sins were forgiven.
Later when we were no longer children
Saturday had a different rhythm,
a slow beginning on the margins of idleness.
Whenever the sky was dismal, a black cloud
dimming the backyards of Pimlico
there was nothing to do but stay home
with the radio on, listen to another
heart-bursting song, Joni singing *Both Sides Now*.
Or in the pale sunshine head downtown
to the citizens' playground, get lost in the crowd,
hangout with a dear companion or two,
see the marchers with banners that said:
Time to stop the unjust distribution of wealth.

2

If there's a day in the week when the waitress is slow,
her sighs infinitely deep, it's Monday –
first day of the week when the rain,
if it rains, is like shards of shrapnel.
Sunday's leftovers are eaten for lunch,
the Sunday parable already shoved from our minds.
Winter Mondays are the worst,
by four o'clock it's dusk on Black Horse Avenue,
long delays on the motorway.
In the park the dogs stop running and go home to sleep.
The train going west breaks down near Portlaoise.
I tell myself a new day is coming, that tomorrow
I'll sit down and finish my *Sonnet in Plain Speech*.

Blackboard, Chalk and Duster

1

A schoolroom in the '60s, blackboard, chalk
and duster and wonders that never ceased.
To please the gods I learned the grammar
of a sleeping language and with the help of rhymes
memorised the fourteen lines that made a sonnet.
Most days were much the same, a juggling act
with the twenty-six letters of the alphabet.
Pythagoras was to blame for the pounding in my heart.
I sat beside the drummer who was always in trouble
for drumming the desk when he needed a rhythm
to break the monotony of a long afternoon.
It was before the revisionists stole history,
the history teacher stood in a trance of bliss
whenever he spoke of Connolly, Plunkett, Pearse.
In geography class I began my travels.
A journey could be endless across the schoolroom map,
through pages of the atlas, from fishing grounds
to coal mines under wet Welsh hills
or down the streets of Toledo, Salamanca, Cadiz.

*Written for the 200ᵗʰ anniversary of my old secondary
school, James's Street CBS*

2

They blend into memory,
the school desk with the inkwell, the black soutane,
my friend, the butcher's son humming *Let's Twist Again.*
In those days the side gate was opened at three o'clock
and we went running to the doughnut shop.

I returned again to that childhood school,
saw my name inscribed on a page
from the year Gagarin became the first man in space
while here on earth prayers were offered
for those on the wrong side of the Berlin Wall.

The ledger had names in Gaelic but the faces
they should have prompted were too faded to dredge from memory.
And after the classroom song and welcoming ceremony
when I saw those hands in the air
I remembered there are questions I have no answer for.

On returning to my primary school in Francis Street 50 years later

The Book of Irish Wars

I asked for the Book of Irish Wars, opened it
and felt the breath of England on my face,
remembered history lessons from school days –
the Tudor age, the curse of Cromwell
and famous battles. The teacher's list was long:
Kinsale, Aughrim, the Boyne and Vinegar Hill,
but most of all his praise was for the seven
whose names were given to seven towers
at the edge of the city. It was only the keepers
of tradition who honoured them
while others whispered their derisions
and wondered why such men were garlanded
for what they did, the fires they lit.
No mention then of the Easter widows:
Grace and Maud, Kathleen, Muriel, Aine, Lillie, Agnes.
A roll-call you could sing to the tune of any rebel ballad.

Tonight the Snowflakes, Tomorrow the Slush

All through the house the radiators
warm up the radiator dust.
December hyacinths are starting to die,
there's a loose stitch I must mend in the coat
I wear through wintertime, the glacial mornings,
the jewelled evenings of January.
Another year makes its exit,
I make a list of things I want to forget.
The first is this: the cruelty of a friend's illness
(I could barely hear his farewell whispers
when he was in the thick of it).
That inch of snow is beginning to rise.
A door blows open admitting a chill, a flower
drops a petal, a dress falls from its hanger,
the calendar slips from a nail in the wall.
Outside in the shrubbery the birds sound anxious.
They see through the enchantment
of snow on the ground, snow on the branches.
Risking the high jump, dropping like lead
the old tomcat with battle scars is young again.

Minding the Shop

in memory of my godfather, Peter Keating

It was a summer job, minding the shop.
The days were long waiting for six o'clock.
To pass the time I scooped sugar from the sugar sack,
bagged it in brown paper bags.
The grocer was a man of local knowledge
who took me to my first shoot-out,
a cowboy flick in the house of red seats.
On Sundays when the mercury was up
he got behind the wheel to drive
into the mountains for a picnic in the pines.
Time and *Newsweek* were his informants
on the world and all its flux.
He told me I should read and learn from them
what school would never teach me,
that news was history happening here-and-now,
that rings a bell we must listen to.
He wanted to save his old town streets
from the wrecking ball, demolition mob.
In City Hall no one listened.
He walked tall in the footsteps of Swift,
through a parish of broken walls, streets half-gone.
In long shopcoat he sold bread and milk
to widows and wives eager to hear him speak
of his seafaring days, every port-of-call, every ocean crossed.

Olympians

And I too have my *beautiful lofty things*,
my Olympians: the teacher
who introduced us to crazed *Macbeth*,
who conjured rainy Inverness
on a Dublin afternoon: I owe him
more gratitude that I possess.
The man from down the street,
an old soldier without a war.
In my childhood he had to wait all week
for his Sunday walk to the river.
The four who gave us Mersey rhythms
and the troubadour accused
of betraying old traditions.
My artist of the west swapped his bog
and shoreline for The Yellow River,
painted it in memory colours.
Two poets: both servants of the state.
One joined the barricades
to defend a city's birthplace.
The other fought a good fight too
and sang through all his suffering.
In the book I cannot rewrite
there are fathers, mothers, aunts and uncles
who had no honeymoon or holiday in the sun.
My Olympians are many but I single out just one:
My Pallas Athena,
she with whom I have come this far,
the place where we take the turn for Ithaca.

Small Talk

for Pauline

At night we talk about the day.
The small catastrophes,
what we let slip through our hands.
And if the day was uneventful
we talk about something else – a book
that won't let us forget its pages of suspense.
You might tell me I am out of touch
because I can't understand the fuss
about Taylor Swift, why all the kids love her.
It's never a long conversation,
sometimes no more than a question and answer.
We might disagree on which of us
asked the other to dance
or the number of days we were snowbound
because our first house was on high ground.
Or you might recall a Sunday drive
to go blackberry-picking on the banks
of the Boyne, a holiday taking our ease
on the sands of Rossnowlagh
or maybe that evening we had the Danube
to ourselves and after making love you led the way,
more by intuition than by reading the map –
down to river where the water was calm,
the fireflies phosphorescent in the dark.

www.ingramcontent.com/pod-product-compliance
Lightning Source LLC
Chambersburg PA
CBHW030500100426
42813CB00002B/291